PICTURING THE PAST
Greece

JOHN MALAM

FRANKLIN WATTS
LONDON•SYDNEY

Titles in this series:
Egypt
Greece
Mesopotamia
Rome

© 2004 Arcturus Publishing Ltd

Produced for Franklin Watts by
Arcturus Publishing Ltd
26/27 Bickels Yard
151-153 Bermondsey Street
London SE1 3HA.

Series concept: Alex Woolf
Editors: Liz Gogerly, Margot Richardson
Designer: Simon Borrough
Picture researcher: Shelley Noronha,
                    Glass Onion Pictures

Published in the UK by Franklin Watts.

A CiP catalogue record for this book is available
from the British Library.

ISBN: 0 7496 5453 8

Printed and bound in Italy

Franklin Watts – the Watts Publishing Group,
96 Leonard Street, London EC2A 4XD.

Picture Acknowledgements:
AKG/Erich Lessing 7 (left), /John Hios 12
(left); Ancient Art and Architecture Collection
Ltd 10 (bottom); The Art Archive /Museo
Nazionale Taranto/Dagli Orti (A) cover, /Dagli
Orti 5, /Epigraphical Museum Athens/Dagli
Orti (A) 9 (left), /Musée du Louvre Paris/Dagli
Orti 9 (right), /Agora Museum Athens/Dagli
Orti 13, /Archaeological Museum
Syracuse/Dagli Orti 15, /Dagli Orti 17 (top),
/Bibliothèque des Arts Décoratifs Paris/Dagli
Orti 17 (bottom), /Museo della Civilta Romana
Rome/Dagli Orti 19, /Museo Nationale Terme
Rome/Dagli Orti 20 (left), /Dagli Orti 21,
/Museo Nazionale Taranto/Dagli Orti (A) 22
(left), /Dagli Orti 23, /Archaeological Museum
Salonica/Dagli Orti (A) 24 (left), /Acropolis
Museum Athens/ Dagli Orti 25, /British
Museum/Eileen Tweedy 27.
Peter Bull Art Studio cover, title page, 3, 4, 8, 10
(top), 11, 12 (right), 18, 20 (right), 22 (right),
24 (right), 28, 29; The Salariya Book Company
Ltd 6, 7 (right), 14, 16, 26.

Note to parents and teachers
Every effort has been made by the publishers to
ensure that these websites are suitable for
children; that they are of the highest educational
value; and that they contain no inappropriate or
offensive material. However, because of the
nature of the Internet, it is impossible to
guarantee that the contents of these sites will
not be altered. We strongly advise that Internet
access is supervised by a responsible adult.

Contents

Landscape

Greece is a country in south-eastern Europe. It lies at the eastern end of the Mediterranean Sea. The ancient Greeks called their country *Hellas*, and the Romans called it *Graecia*, from which comes our word 'Greece'. It is a country made up of a mainland part joined to Europe, and about 2,000 islands in the Aegean, Ionian, and Mediterranean seas.

The mainland of Greece is rugged, with mountain ranges covering almost three-quarters of the land. Fertile plains and valleys lie between the mountains. The islands, which are as rocky as the mainland, vary greatly in size. Crete is the largest island. Today, as in the past, most islands are uninhabited.

This was the landscape the ancient Greeks knew. They were well aware of the geography of their land, which they wrote about in books and plays. For example, Plato (c. 427-347BCE), a Greek philosopher, wrote: 'The earth is very vast, and we live around the sea like frogs around a pond'. This is a famous quotation. Plato was comparing the

GREECE
The mainland of Greece is a peninsula, surrounded on three sides by sea. The mainland has about 15,000 km of coastline. Nowhere in Greece is more than 130 km from the coast.

HOW DO WE KNOW?

There are several ways to find out about ancient Greece. One method is to read the words of the Greeks themselves. Many of their books and plays have survived, giving eyewitness stories of their world. Also, inscriptions carved on stone monuments, or paintings on pottery, are other first-hand ways of finding out about the Greeks. Another type of evidence comes out of the ground. This is information from archaeological excavations, where the remains of the past are uncovered and studied. Archaeologists are detectives, gathering together a mass of information, from which they can work out facts that cannot be learned any other way.

HIGHEST PEAK

The tallest mountain in Greece is called Mount Olympus (2,918 metres). The ancient Greeks believed it was the home of their twelve most important gods. They were named the Olympian gods, after the mountain.

Greeks, who lived close to the sea, with frogs, who never move far from their home pond.

Strabo (c. 64BCE-CE21), a Greek geographer, put it another way. He said: 'The sea presses in upon the country with a thousand arms'. This was his way of describing the jagged coastline of Greece, with its many inlets and sea channels.

Although the history of Greece can be traced back for thousands of years, this book is only concerned with a short time known as the 'Classical Age' (about 480-323BCE). It was a time when Greek culture was at its richest, and when one city, Athens, was supreme.

Some things today can be traced back to the ancient Greeks, such as freedom of speech, democracy, theatre, and the Olympic Games. They affect our lives, which is why it is important to learn about the people who created them.

WEBLINK
http://www.settlement.org/cp/english/greece/landclim.html

At-a-glance facts about the landscape and climate of Greece.

5

Farming

GOATS
Most farms had goats. Their milk was drunk fresh, or made into a sharp-tasting soft cheese. At festival times, goats were sacrificed as gifts to please the gods.

WEBLINK

http://oncampus.richmond. edu/academics/as/ education/projects/ webunits/greecerome/ Greeceag1.html

All about farming and farmers in ancient Greece.

Farming was an essential part of everyday life for most people in ancient Greece. Those who lived in the countryside, away from busy towns and cities, worked on the land. Farmers were respected and highly valued members of society. The food they produced and took to market fed the population, and their linen, wool, and leather became the clothes that people wore.

In the countryside around the city of Athens, farms were an average size of about 4-8 hectares. This is tiny by today's standards, but 2,300 years ago it was a good size for a farm, where all the work was done by hand with the aid of simple machines and draught animals.

The farming year began in October, when farmers ploughed their fields. Oxen pulled ploughs through the stony soil, breaking it up to be planted. Wheat (for bread) and barley (for bread and porridge) were the main cereal crops, which grew through the mild winter and were harvested in May.

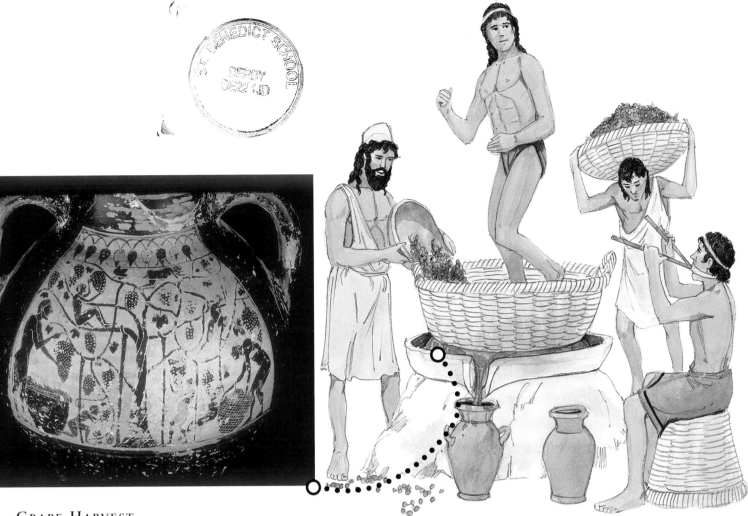

GRAPE HARVEST

The scene painted on this ancient Greek *amphora* shows men and boys gathering bunches of grapes at harvest time. Wooden supports hold up the vine, and the picked grapes are put into wicker baskets.

Peas, leeks, onions, beans and lettuces were the main vegetables. Several types of fruit were grown, including apples, pears, pomegranates and figs. Most important of all were grapes, which were made into wine or eaten fresh, and olives, which gave oil for cooking and for burning in lamps to give light. The Greeks were famous for their olive oil, and it was exported to other lands.

Farmers raised sheep, goats, cattle, pigs and poultry. They provided wool, hides, eggs, meat and milk (used fresh or made into cheese). Bees were kept for their honey.

WINE-MAKING

Ripe grapes were picked in September. The fruit was trodden to squeeze out the juice, which was stored in pottery jars for six months. During this time natural sugars in the grape juice fermented and it turned into wine. It was ready to drink in March.

HOW DO WE KNOW?

We are lucky to have a long poem about Greek agriculture. It was written about 700BCE, by Hesiod, a farmer-poet, and it is called *Work and Days*. As well, archaeologists have found vases painted with farming scenes, and tools such as plough shares (blades), sickles for cutting, sieves for straining, and presses for squeezing. Farm buildings and fields have been excavated, and crops have been identified from their preserved pollen and seeds.

Education

In the main city of Greece, Athens, there were different types of education for boys and girls.

Most boys went to school from the age of seven. Boys in Athens were expected to grow into responsible citizens of the city-state, so it was important for them to learn how to read, write, and work with numbers. They were also taught to sing and play musical instruments, especially the lyre, and had physical education lessons, teaching them to be strong and brave.

Teachers, who were always men, set examples for boys to follow. Poetry, speeches, and long passages from plays were memorized. Students had tests to find out how much they remembered. School rooms were often in teachers' homes. Boys were taken there by slaves who worked for their families. They stayed with them to make sure they did their work.

WEBLINK

http://members.aol.com/ Donnclass/Greeklife. html#EDUCATION

Learn more about Greek education, and compare the systems in Athens and Sparta.

GREEK SCHOOL
Boys learned to write by copying words onto wax-coated wooden tablets. At the end of a lesson the soft wax was smoothed out, and the tablet was re-used.

Parents had to pay for boys' education. Rich families could afford school until their sons were eighteen years old. These boys went from elementary school to schools where they studied philosophy or public speaking. Boys from poorer families only went for three or four years, and were given only a basic education.

GREEK WRITING
From about 750BCE the ancient Greeks began using a writing system composed of twenty-six letters. The first two letters were named *alpha* and *beta*, from which comes the word 'alphabet'. Some are seen here, carved into a stone.

GIRLS WEAVING
Clothes were made at home by women. They used wool (from sheep) or linen (from the flax plant). This painting, on the side of a vase, shows girls spinning raw fibres: twisting them into long threads which could be woven into cloth.

Girls in Athens rarely went to school. Most stayed at home where their mothers taught them women's duties, such as preparing food, weaving wool, and making clothes. It trained them for married life, when they would have to look after their own homes.

Girls may have learned a little reading and writing, but this was not considered important for them.

HOW DO WE KNOW?

Evidence of education comes from many sources. Greek poets and playwrights wrote about it. For example, in his play called *Clouds*, Aristophanes (c. 455-386BCE) compared old methods of education with ones that came into fashion in the 400s BCE. In the old system, emphasis was placed on physical education and music, whereas the new system made reading, writing, and number work more important. We can also learn about Greek education from objects. Pictures painted on vases show teachers and students; writing pens and tablets have survived; and there are numerous examples of actual writing – proof that people were educated.

Slaves

HOUSEHOLD SLAVE
Female slaves mainly worked in people's homes. Their duties ranged from cleaning and cooking to washing and weaving. Like slaves everywhere, they had to obey their owner's instructions.

USEFUL TOOLS
Slaves were little more than 'useful tools', employed as their owners wished. Male slaves, who worked in their owner's home one day, could be sent to work in his fields the next day. This woman is grinding some grain.

HOW DO WE KNOW?

Our knowledge of ancient Greek slavery is based on the writings of Greek philosophers, playwrights and historians such as Aristotle (c. 384-322BCE) and Plato. It is from them that we are able to understand why slavery was considered both an acceptable and a normal state for a person to be in. Far from slavery being seen as cruel or disrespectful, which is the view of the modern world, the Greeks saw a slave's whole existence as a gift from his or her master. It was the master who had saved the slave from an unfortunate former life, and had given him or her food and shelter.

Slaves were common in ancient Greece. To give you an idea of how many there were, in the 400s BCE almost half the population of Attica (the city of Athens and countryside under its control) were slaves. That's 100,000 slaves out of a population of about 250,000 people.

Prisoners of war, criminals and victims of slave raids were all likely to end up being sold into a life of slavery in Greece. This happened to men, women and children. Whatever their background, they all had one thing in common – none of them were Greek. The idea of Greeks enslaving fellow Greeks was considered deeply offensive. Such respect was not shown to non-Greeks – foreigners were looked down on as natural slaves.

Greek traders bought and sold slaves in markets, like other goods. The island of Delos was the centre of the slave trade, and as many as 1,000 slaves were sold there every day.

In Athens even the poorest citizen owned a slave, while the richest had as many as fifty. Most slaves were bought to work in people's homes. Some were bought as investments, and were rented out to work in workshops or mines in return for a payment to their owners. Others belonged to the city of Athens and worked as clerks in public buildings, as coin-testers on the lookout for fakes, or as police whose job was to keep the peace in the city.

Masters beat their slaves if they misbehaved, but they could not kill them. When they could no longer work, through illness or old age, loyal slaves were cared for by their masters and were treated like members of the family.

WEBLINK
http://www.crystalinks.com/greekslavery.html

Slavery in ancient Greece, with facts about the duties of slaves, and special reference to women slaves.

MINE SLAVES
The city of Athens owned mines at Laurium, where valuable silver ore was quarried from narrow passages and chambers underground. The 20,000 slaves who worked here belonged to the city, or were hired out by private owners. Work continued night and day, with slaves working ten-hour shifts without a break. This was the worst job for a slave.

Democracy

The ancient Greeks devised a form of government they called *demokratia*, from which comes our word 'democracy'. Meaning 'the rule of the people', democracy arose in Athens in the 400s BCE. It was a system of government in which ordinary adult male citizens (not women, foreigners or slaves) became involved in the day-to-day administration and politics of Athens.

ASSEMBLY

Male citizens of Athens, aged twenty and over, met forty times a year. These were meetings of the people's Assembly, or *ekklesia*. Citizens listened to speeches which described plans the city Council had for Athens. When the speakers had finished, the citizens voted for or against the Council by raising their hands. The decision of the Assembly was final – the people had spoken. This was democracy in action.

MEETING PLACE

In Athens, meetings of the Assembly were usually held on the Pnyx hill, but they could also be held in the city's *agora* (marketplace). At least 6,000 citizens had to attend, or an Assembly could not go ahead. At the Pnyx, speakers made their speeches from a stone rostrum, or platform, cut into the hill.

WEBLINK
http://www.historyforkids.
org/learn/greeks/
government/index.htm

Facts about different
types of government,
including democracy, in
ancient Greece.

Democracy in Athens was a two-part system. One part was the Council, or *boule*. It was a group of 500 male citizens aged thirty and over. They held daily meetings in the council hall (*bouleuterion*). Each man could only be a city councillor for one year at a time, after which another man took his place.

The council hall was a debating chamber. It was a square building with sides 23 metres long, inside which were tiers of stone benches on three sides. Councillors sat on the benches while a speaker addressed them from the floor of the chamber. When he had finished, another man took his turn at speaking. Questions were called out, and the speaker answered them as best, and as persuasively, as he could.

One of the Council's main functions was to debate issues that affected Athens. These included proposals for new laws, or changes to existing ones, money matters, the construction of public buildings, dealings with other cities in Greece, and threats posed by enemies.

At the end of a Council meeting an agenda was drawn up for the Assembly – the second part of the democratic process in Athens. At an Assembly meeting the plans of the Council were announced to ordinary male citizens. The Assembly then held its own debate, at the end of which they voted to accept or reject the proposals the Council had put to them.

LEAVE TOWN
An unpopular man, usually a politician, could be forced to leave Athens. Every male citizen had the chance to cast one vote for the man they wanted thrown out. Names were scratched onto pieces of pottery called *ostraka*, from which comes our word 'ostracize' (to banish). As long as at least 6,000 votes were cast, the man with the most votes was ostracized. He had to leave Athens for ten years. This *ostrakon* has the name 'Aristides, son of Lysimachus' on it.

HOW DO WE KNOW?

Our knowledge of Greek democracy, particularly the way it was practised in Athens, comes from a variety of sources. The works of Greek writers, such as the great statesman Demosthenes (384-322BCE), are particularly valuable, as their books and speeches contain a wealth of information about the workings of democracy. Excavations in the heart of Athens have uncovered thousands of *ostraka*, on which we can read the names of men who were banished from the city by public vote, and the meeting place of the Assembly, on the Pnyx hill, survives almost intact.

Religion

THE TWELVE
OLYMPIANS
Apollo: sun god
Aphrodite: love goddess
Ares: war god
Artemis: moon goddess
Athena: war goddess
Demeter: farming
goddess
Hephaestus: fire god
Hera: queen of the gods
* Dionysus: wine god
Hermes: travel god
Poseidon: sea god
Zeus: king of the gods

* In early lists of the
twelve Olympian gods,
Hestia, the hearth
goddess, was
included. However, as
time passed her
popularity and
importance faded, and
her place was taken by
Dionysus, the wine god.

The ancient Greeks worshipped many different gods and goddesses. People imagined them as super-human beings who had great powers (such as being able to control the weather, or change their shape), but who also had human weaknesses (such as anger and jealousy).

There was no such thing as a 'national religion' with rules that everyone followed, like some modern faiths. Each town had its own patron deity. For example, Athena was worshipped in the cities of Athens and Sparta, Hera in Argos, and Apollo in Delphi. Each deity was thought to control a different aspect

WEBLINK
http://www.mythweb.
com

All the heroes, gods,
goddesses and monsters
of Greek mythology.

GODDESS OF LOVE

Aphrodite was the goddess of love and beauty. She had the power to make ordinary people and her fellow gods fall in love with each other. She is pictured on this pottery vase looking at her reflection in a mirror, admiring her own beauty.

of life. Because of this, people chose to worship the god or goddess they thought would be most useful to them at any given time. A proverb said: 'Gifts persuade the gods'. It was a simple idea. People wanted their gifts to please the gods, and in return they hoped their prayers would be answered. A gift could be a prayer itself, or something 'real', such as food and clothing, or an animal sacrifice.

HOW DO WE KNOW?

We know much about Greek gods and goddesses thanks to stories about them. These stories, or myths, were passed on by word of mouth until eventually they were written down. The works of poets such as Homer and Hesiod (both lived in the 700s BCE) are full of details about the birth of the gods, their relationships to one another, their deeds, and links with humans. And we can see what the Greeks thought their gods and goddesses looked like because of the many stone and metal statues and vase paintings that have been found.

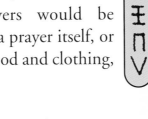

The most important deities were a family of twelve gods and goddesses, said to live on the snowy summit of Mount Olympus which seemed to reach all the way up to heaven. They were named the Olympians after their mountain home. These major deities were worshipped in towns and sacred sanctuaries throughout the Greek world (Greece and the area beyond, where Greek culture had spread to).

In addition, people believed in lesser beings known as nymphs. They were female spirits who represented the beauty of nature, such as trees and streams. Nymphs were the equivalent of fairies: shy, secretive creatures who kept well away from humans. They, too, needed to be pleased. People left gifts for them in places where they thought they might dwell, such as caves and forest clearings.

15

Festivals

THE ACROPOLIS

At the heart of ancient Athens was the Acropolis hill. It was the religious centre of the city, where temples, altars and sacred statues stood. The largest and most famous temple on the hill was the Parthenon. It was built from marble. Inside was a statue of Athena 12 metres high, made from gold, ivory and timber.

Festivals were an important feature of religion and also of sport (see page 20). They were both holy days and holidays. Because the week was not divided into work and rest days, as our week is, a festival was when people could relax and spend time with family and friends. It was also a time to thank the town's patron god or goddess, honouring and celebrating the deity who watched over and protected the population.

Religious festivals were not national events, as ours are today. Instead, they were local celebrations. Every town and city in Greece had its own yearly cycle of festivals. In Athens, festivals began in the month of Hecatombaion (July-August), with the festival of Cronia (at which masters and slaves shared a meal together), and with the most important festival, the Panathenaea (see right). In the month of Pyanepsion (September-October) four festivals took place in Athens, including one for women only. This was the three-day festival of Thesmophoria, in honour of Demeter, goddess of farming. During the festival women fasted (ate no food) and offered sacrifices of piglets and corn to the goddess. It was a fertility

festival, designed to give thanks to the goddess for providing food.

The Panathenaea was the greatest of all festivals in Athens. It was held in celebration of Athena, the city's patron goddess. The city was named in her honour, and the festival was held on the goddess's birthday, the 28th day of Hecatombaion. The festival culminated in a grand procession to the top of the Acropolis hill and the Parthenon temple, taking with it a new robe (*peplos*) which was to be presented to the goddess. In a ceremony on the hilltop, the robe was draped over the ancient olive-wood statue of Athena. Then came a great sacrifice of one hundred cows and some sheep, followed by feasting.

Once every four years a Great Panathenaea festival was held. It lasted for twelve days, and included sacrifices and feasts, together with contests for singing, dancing and athletics.

A GOD'S HOME

A temple, such as the Parthenon in Athens (above), was the most important religious building in a town. It represented the earthly home of the town's patron god or goddess. The deity's spirit was believed to live within the statue kept inside the building. In the sacred enclosure outside the temple was an altar, where worshippers offered gifts to the deity.

WEBLINK
http://depthome.
brooklyn.cuny.edu/
classics/dunkle/athnlife/
rligious.htm

Find out all about the
Panathenaea festival.

SACRIFICE

Animals were sacrificed to the gods on temple altars. Their necks were cut and they bled to death. Some meat was then burnt on the altar fire as a gift to the gods. The rest was cooked and eaten by worshippers and priests. Sheep and goats were the usual sacrificial animals. Bulls, as in the picture below, were the greatest of all gifts to the gods.

HOW DO WE KNOW?

Ancient Greek writers described festivals. The historian Thucydides (c. 460-400BCE) said of them: 'When our work is over, we are in a position to enjoy all kinds of recreation for our spirits.' He was saying that festivals offered people a welcome break from their daily routines. Physical evidence for festivals also exists. Carved in marble panels that once ran around the top of the Parthenon temple in Athens is a detailed frieze. It shows the procession in the city's yearly Panathenaea festival.

17

Medicine

BLOOD-LETTING
Greek doctors who practised scientific, or Hippocratic, medicine believed a person's sickness could be diagnosed by studying bodily fluids, such as blood, bile and phlegm. They also thought (wrongly) that a person could be cured if they were bled – letting a quantity of blood drain from the body.

Two types of medicine were practised in ancient Greece: temple medicine and scientific medicine.

The older of the two types was temple medicine, which was associated with Asclepius, the god of healing. During the 400s and 300s BCE, people from across the Greek world travelled to his temple at Epidaurus, on the mainland of Greece. It was a large and busy sanctuary. As the sick slept inside the temple precincts they hoped Asclepius would come to them in their dreams and would speak to them.

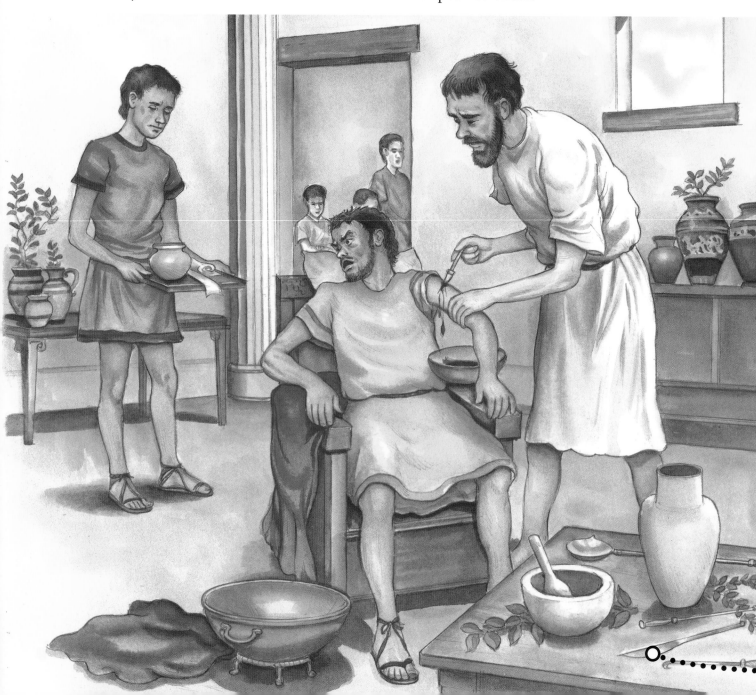

DOCTOR'S KIT
Carved on this stone is a set of implements used by a Greek doctor. In the centre is a hinged box containing his knives and probes, which would have been made from bronze. Either side of the box is a glass cup, used in a procedure known as 'cupping'. This was when blood was drawn, or sucked, out of the body and collected in cups like these.

Next morning they described their dreams to the temple's priests. The priests interpreted the dreams and explained what treatment Asclepius had prescribed. This could be the reciting prayers, wearing protective amulets (charms), or taking herb medicines.

Temple medicine was a spiritual or magical experience, since a person felt they had been in the god's presence. The power of faith may have been enough to cure some people. Perhaps miracles happened at the healing centre at Epidaurus.

The second type of medicine had a scientific approach. Doctors observed the sick, diagnosed their problems, then prescribed a range of practical remedies. This is how doctors work today.

Medicine of this type is known as Hippocratic medicine, after Hippocrates (c. 460-390BCE), a Greek doctor called the 'father of medicine'. Doctors who followed his teachings believed diseases had natural causes, which could be cured by natural means, such as massage, changes to diet, fasting, exercising and sulphur baths. They also used ointments and did blood-letting.

WEBLINK
http://www.mnsu.edu/ emuseum/prehistory/ aegean/culture/ greekmedicine.html

An outline of medicine in ancient Greece, with the text of the Hippocratic Oath, taken by doctors.

HOW DO WE KNOW?

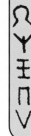

Our knowledge of Greek medicine is both historical and archaeological. Many medical texts written by the Greeks have survived, and by reading these we can find out how scientific doctors worked and what they believed. Examples of doctors' medical equipment have also been found. At Epidaurus, the healing centre of Asclepius has been excavated, and many offerings left by ancient visitors have been found. These include models of body parts, such as arms and legs. They were gifts to Asclepius, either as grateful thanks for a cure received, or in the hope of cure to come.

Sport

Festivals of sport were staged at regular intervals in ancient Greece. They were held in honour of a god, which meant they were a type of religious festival (see page 14). However, unlike town festivals which were specific to certain places, sports festivals were national events, recognized throughout the Greek world. There were four such festivals. The most important was the Olympic Games, held at Olympia in the west of Greece, in honour of Zeus, the king of the gods. The first Olympic Games were held in 776BCE.

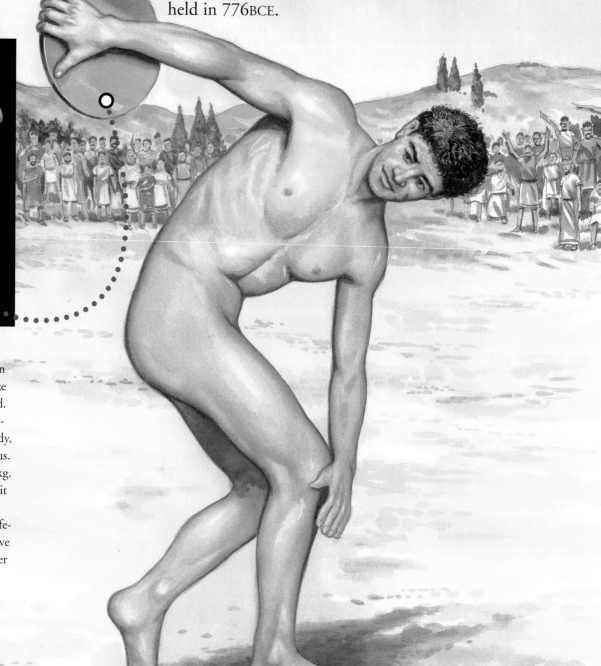

THE DISCUS

In the discus event an athlete threw a bronze disc as far as he could. He made a fast three-quarter turn of his body, then released the discus. It weighed about 2.5 kg. The man who threw it the furthest was the winner. The ancient life-size marble statue above shows a discus-thrower in action.

EVENTS AT THE OLYMPIC GAMES

Day 1
- opening ceremony
- public and private sacrifices
- boys' running, wrestling and boxing contests

Day 2
- chariot races
- horse races
- pentathlon (running, discus, jumping, javelin, wrestling)
- parade of winners
- singing of hymns

Day 3
- the main sacrifices
- foot races
- public banquet

Day 4
- wrestling
- boxing
- *pankration* (boxing, kicking and wrestling combined)
- race in armour

Day 5
- winners receive wreaths
- closing ceremony
- feasting

The Olympic Games were held once every four years. They lasted for five days and included gymnastics, athletics and events with horses. Men from all over Greece competed in track and field activities (see box). Athletes and gymnasts competed naked, but horse-riders and charioteers wore clothes. Victors brought honour to their towns and cities, and to themselves. They were awarded crowns of olive leaves and palm fronds. Women held a separate festival at Olympia. This was the Heraean Games, in honour of the goddess Hera. There was just one event – a track race for girls.

WEBLINK
http://www.bbc.co.uk/ schools/landmarks/ ancientgreece/olympia/ index.shtml

The ancient Olympic Games, with facts about Olympia, the sporting events, and more.

THE WAY IN
Contestants and judges entered the stadium at Olympia through a tunnel. It was 32 metres long with an arched roof, part of which still survives. The tunnel was originally buried out of sight under a bank of soil. Because it was so well hidden, an ancient writer called it a 'secret entrance'.

HOW DO WE KNOW?

Sporting festivals are known about because writers described them. For example, Pausanias (writing in the CE 100s) is a source of information on Olympia and the Olympic Games. He described a gold and ivory statue of Zeus, some 13 metres high, seated inside the temple at Olympia. It was one of the Seven Wonders of the World. Though nothing remains of the statue, the temple which was once its home, together with much of Olympia, has been excavated. In addition to uncovering Olympia's ground plan, statues of athletes have been found, together with equipment such as discusses, and *haltares* (weights that helped an athlete jump further).

Theatre

All the parts in a play were performed by men – there were no actresses. The men wore painted masks made from wood, cork or stiffened linen, tied to their heads with cords, or fitted like helmets. Masks showed the audience the part the actor was playing, and the mood he was in.

MASK
A mask worn by an actor performing a funny part in a comedy.

The ancient Greeks had a form of entertainment which we enjoy today – the theatre. It has its origins in a festival held in honour of Dionysus, the god of wine. In Athens, the festival was held each March when, for four days, groups of male actors (each group was called a *chorus*) competed with each other by performing dances and songs in the *agora* (the city marketplace). Judges gave prizes to the winning group. In time, plays were specially written for actors to perform at the City Dionysia, as the festival was known. This was the start of theatre in Greece.

There were two types of plays: comedies and tragedies. In a comedy, actors performed scenes from everyday life, often making fun of top politicians and other leaders. It was easy for the audience to follow, and was fun to watch. A tragedy was different. Here, actors performed scenes from myths, telling stories about gods and goddesses, and heroic men and women. A tragedy was a serious play, usually with a sad ending.

22

THEATRE

A theatre was an open-air building. The audience sat on tiers of stone seats arranged in a semi-circle around a circular area of beaten earth or sand. The actors performed on this area, called the *orchestra*. The theatre at Epidaurus, seen here, could seat 12,000 spectators. It is still used for plays today.

Plays were staged in the daytime, in theatres often built inside bowl-shaped hollows in the landscape. This shape allowed actors' voices to carry easily to the back seats. Also, actors' masks had wide, funnel-shaped mouths which helped to increase the volume of their voices. Everyone in the audience heard clearly the words being spoken or sung.

Actors usually wore bulky, padded costumes and platform-soled shoes. People sitting far away from the acting area could easily see the actors because of their larger-than-life outfits.

WEBLINK
http://www.bbc.co.uk/
schools/landmarks/
ancientgreece/classics/
theatre/intro.shtml

The theatre in ancient Greece, with facts about the building, actors, plays and audience.

HOW DO WE KNOW?

Plays survive from playwrights such as Aristophanes (c. 450-385BCE) who wrote comedies, and Euripedes (c. 485-406BCE) who wrote tragedies. Theatre buildings exist all over the Greek world, and masks and admission tickets (small bronze discs), together with vases decorated with images of actors, have all been found. Some English words are based on ones the Greeks used – theatre is from *theatron* ('a place for seeing'); drama is from *dran* ('to act, or do'); comedy is from *komoidia* ('to have fun'), and tragedy is from *tragoidia* ('goat-song', perhaps because the first tragedies were sung by actors dressed as satyrs – half human, half goat creatures).

23

Warfare

Wars were fought on land and at sea. Rival city-states fought land battles with armies of foot soldiers called hoplites. At sea, warships called triremes clashed with other enemy ships.

In land battles, fought on flat, open plains, ranks of hoplites stood shield-to-shield in a formation called a phalanx. It was six to eight ranks deep, with hundreds of men in each rank. In battle, opposing phalanxes marched or ran towards each other.

HELMET
The helmet of a Greek foot soldier. It is made from one sheet of bronze metal, beaten into shape. The soldier's head, neck, nose and cheeks were well protected.

HOPLITE
A Greek foot soldier was called a hoplite, after his *hoplon*, or shield. He was armed with a spear and sword. His body armour was a bronze breastplate and greaves (leg guards).

The first three ranks of men held their spears level, pointing them at the enemy. The soldiers behind carried their spears point upward. When the armies met, the front soldiers thrust their spears into each other's phalanx, while the men in the back ranks pushed their comrades forward toward the enemy.

WEBLINK
http://www.holycross.
edu/departments/
classics/dawhite/

The Greek hoplite soldier – what he wore and what it was like to fight in battle.

WARSHIP
This carving, in marble, shows oarsmen rowing a a warship. A trireme (so-named because it had three rows of oarsmen) was powered by about 170 men. It was about 37 metres long, yet only about 5 metres wide. This long, narrow shape was perfect for speeding through the water.

A Greek land battle was a contest of physical strength. The idea was to push so hard that the weaker of the two sides would lose its formation. Its phalanx would break up, and its soldiers would flee the battlefield.

At sea, battles also relied on brute force. A Greek trireme was armed with a battering ram. Fitted to the front of the vessel at the waterline, it was made from wood sheathed in thick bronze. In battle, triremes aimed to ram each other, holing the enemy ship and sinking it. About ten hoplites and archers were carried on board a Greek trireme, positioned on the narrow deck above the oarsmen. Their job was to engage the enemy at close range, firing arrows.

HOW DO WE KNOW?
Many examples of ancient Greek metal armour and weapons have been found, from which it is possible to reconstruct the battledress of a hoplite soldier. Vase paintings show what patterns were painted on their shields, and how crests, made of horse-hair, looked on their helmets. Although no wrecks of trireme warships have yet been located, a bronze battering ram has been found off the coast of Israel, dated to c. 200BCE. It is a type that would have been used by Greek warships. Sculptures and vase paintings give clues as to how warships looked. A full-scale replica of a trireme has been built, helping historians to understand these ancient vessels in detail.

Crafts

A WEBLINK

http://www.museum.
upenn.edu/Greek_
World/pottery_images.
html

Online exhibit from
the University of
Pennsylvania Museum
of Archaeology and
Anthropology,
showing a gallery of
Greek pottery.

There were many different crafts in ancient Greece. Craftworkers turned raw materials into a range of items, including jewellery, glass, leatherwork, textiles, mosaics and paintings. Stone, clay and metal were common materials, and some of the objects made are described here.

Quarries provided stone such as limestone and marble, from which sculptors carved life-like statues of gods, people and animals, and also reliefs (decorated stone slabs). Stonemasons made columns and blocks for buildings. Both types of stone workers used bronze and iron tools. To make a marble statue, heavy chisels and punches first roughed out the shape, then finer ones smoothed the surface. Abrasive powder from a hard

WORKSHOPS
Most Greek towns had a district packed with craftworkers' workshops, located away from residential areas where people lived. Workshops were busy places, where raw materials were brought to and finished goods were sent out from. Some districts specialized in just one craft, such as pottery-making.

POTTERY

Most people could not afford metal jugs and vases, so they had ones made from pottery (oven-baked clay). Potters produced a vast range of different shaped vessels, from cups and bowls to storage jars for wine and oil, such as this *amphora*. Some pots were decorated with scenes from mythology; others were left plain.

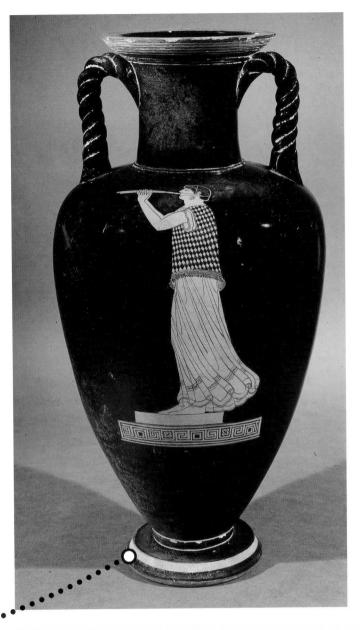

mineral called emery was rubbed over the surface to polish it and remove all traces of tool marks. Last of all, the statue was painted in bright life-like colours, then coated in a layer of wax and oil to protect the paintwork. As we look at these statues today, all we see is the natural colour of the stone – the paint wore off long ago.

Bronze was also used to make statues, as well as useful items ranging from jugs and mirrors to swords and armour. Today, ancient bronze objects appear a dull greenish-brown colour, but when they were new they were a shiny yellow.

The craftworkers of ancient Greece learned their trades in the workshops of masters, and their knowledge was passed down from one generation to the next.

HOW DO WE KNOW?

Much of our knowledge for the crafts of the Greeks is based on archaeological evidence. Statues made from metal and stone have been found at sites throughout the Greek world, and some have been recovered from shipwrecks in the Mediterranean and Aegean seas. Thousands of pots have been discovered amongst the ruins of buildings, rare paintings are found on the walls of tombs, and precious items of gold jewellery sometimes come to light. Archaeologists, historians, artists and experts in ancient technology study the objects to find out how they were made, and what they can tell us about the people who made them.

Timeline

A NOTE ABOUT DATES

All the dates in this timeline are BCE dates. This stands for 'before the Common Era'. BCE dates are counted back from the year 1, which is taken to be the beginning of the Common Era (CE). There was no year 0. These dates work in the same way as BC (before Christ) and AD (*Anno Domini*, which means 'the year of our Lord').

Some dates have the letter 'c.' in front of them. This stands for *circa*, which means 'about'. These dates are guesses, because no one knows what the real date is.

THE BRONZE AGE:

c. 3500-1100BCE A time when palaces and fortified towns were built and people lived prosperous lives.

c. 3500BCE The Minoan civilization begins on the island of Crete.

c. 2200BCE The Minoans build palaces, and their civilization flourishes on Crete.

c. 1600BCE The Mycenaean civilization begins on mainland Greece; these people were the first Greeks.

c. 1650BCE The Minoans on Crete use writing, known by scholars as Linear A.

c. 1700BCE Earthquakes destroy the Minoan palaces on Crete; they were rebuilt.

c. 1400BCE Mycenaeans use the first Greek writing, known by scholars as Linear B.

c. 1100BCE The Minoan and Mycenaean civilizations end.

THE DARK AGES:

c. 1100-800BCE A time of unrest, when the art of writing was lost and people lived poorer lives.

c. 1100BCE First use of iron for tools and weapons.

c. 1050-950BCE Some Greeks leave the mainland and settle on Aegean islands

c. 850-750BCE Homer, the greatest Greek poet, lives. He wrote famous long poems called the *Iliad* and the *Odyssey*.

THE ARCHAIC PERIOD:

c. 800-500BCE A time of recovery when people began to feel hopeful again, and the art of writing returned.

c. 750BCE The first Greek alphabet is devised.

c. 750-650BCE People migrate from Greece and settle elsewhere in the Mediterranean and Asia Minor, where they build many Greek cities, such as Neapolis (Naples, Italy), and Massalia (Marseille, France).

776BCE Traditional date of the first Olympic Games, held at Olympia.

660s-630sBCE Trade with Egypt and Africa.

c. 610BCE Black-figure pottery first made.

c. 600BCE First Greek coins are used.

c. 546BCE The Persians conquer Greek colonies in Ionia (Turkey).

c. 535BCE Red-figure pottery first made.

c. 505BCE Democracy is introduced in Athens.

THE CLASSICAL AGE:

c. 500-323BCE A 'golden age', when the Greeks controlled a vast empire and their civilization was at its most advanced.

493BCE Piraeus becomes the port of Athens.

490-480BCE Wars against the Persians; the Greeks are ultimately victorious.

447-38BCE The Parthenon temple built at Athens.

430BCE Plague at Athens.

431-404BCE Athens looses a war with Sparta, another city in Greece.

358-330BCE Theatre of Epidaurus built.

359-336BCE Reign of King Philip II.

338BCE King Philip II becomes the ruler of Greece.

336BCE King Philip II dies. His son, Alexander, takes over from him.

334-323BCE Conquests of Alexander the Great in Persia and further east, creating an empire for Greece.

323BCE Alexander dies, and his empire breaks up.

HELLENISTIC AGE:

323-30BCE The time when the Hellenistic (Greek) empire split into kingdoms, which eventually became part of the Roman world.

279BCE Greece invaded by Gauls.

148BCE Macedonia becomes part of the Roman Empire.

146BCE Mainland Greece becomes part of the Roman Empire.

129BCE Greek cities overseas pass to the Romans.

30BCE Egypt, the last of the Hellenistic (Greek) kingdoms, becomes part of the Roman Empire.

Glossary

Agenda A list of items of business to be dealt with at a meeting.

Agora An open space in a town which served as a marketplace, administrative and social centre.

Amphora A large pot with a narrow neck for storing wine. Its name means 'two handled'.

Archaeologist A person who finds out about the past by looking for the remains of buildings and other objects, often beneath the ground.

Assembly Gathering of the citizens of a Greek town and the land it governed.

BCE Used in dates. Means 'before the Common Era'.

Bronze A hard metal made by mixing copper with tin.

CE Used in dates. Means 'the Common Era'. The Common Era begins with year 1 which is the same as the year AD1 in the Christian calendar.

Cereal A grass, such as wheat or barley, that produces a grain used for food.

Citizen A person with full rights in a country or, as in Ancient Greece, a city and its territory.

City-state A self-governing city and its surrounding land.

Deity A god or goddess; a supreme being.

Democracy A type of government where the people have a say in what happens, usually by electing others to represent them.

Diagnose Identify an illness or the medical condition of someone.

Eyewitness A person who has personally seen something and so can give a first-hand description of it.

Hoplite A heavily armed foot-soldier.

Implements Tools or utensils.

Local Relating to a particular area or neighbourhood.

Lyre A musical instrument with strings fixed in a U-shaped frame.

Marble A hard-wearing stone used for buildings and statues.

Myths Well-known stories about the early history of a people, usually involving supernatural beings or events.

National Relating to an entire nation or country.

Ore Rock from which metal can be extracted.

Ostracize To banish a person from a town; to send a person into exile.

Peninsula An area of land sticking out into the sea or a lake.

Phalanx A war formation of hoplites.

Philosophy The study of knowledge and humankind's existence.

Politics The way in which a government works; its ideas put into practice.

Proverb A well-known saying that states the truth or gives advice.

Sacrifice Killing an animal to please the gods.

Sanctuary A sacred place.

Stadium A sports ground with tiers of seats for people to watch

Vase A container, usually made from pottery, used to hold liquids such as wine, water and oil. It could be plain, or decorated with designs from patterns of lines to scenes showing figures of gods, goddesses and heroes.

Further information

BOOKS ABOUT ANCIENT GREECE

The Ancient City: Life in Classical Athens and Rome by Peter Connolly, and Hazel Dodge (Oxford University Press, 1998)

Ancient Greece by Peter Connolly (Oxford University Press, 2001)

Ancient Greece (Eyewitness Guide) by Anne Pearson (Dorling Kindersley, 2002)

Ancient Greece: Gods and Goddesses by John Malam (Wayland, 1999)

Ancient Greece: Greek Theatre by Stewart Ross (Wayland, 1996)

Ancient Greece: The Original Olympics by Stewart Ross (Wayland, 1999)

Ancient Greeks At A Glance by John Malam (Hodder Wayland, 1998)

The British Museum Illustrated Encyclopedia of Ancient Greece by Sean Sheehan (British Museum Press, 2002)

The Greeks by Susan Peach and Anne Millard (Usborne, 1995)

The Greeks (Rebuilding the Past) by Roy Burrell (Oxford University Press, 1990)

History Starts Here: The Ancient Greeks by John Malam (Wayland, 1999)

Metropolis: Greek Town by John Malam (Franklin Watts, 2000)

Pinpoints: An Ancient Greek Temple by John Malam (Hodder Wayland, 2002)

The Usborne Encyclopedia of Ancient Greece by Jane Chisholm, Lisa Miles and Struan Reid (Usborne, 2003)

BOOKS ABOUT THE GREEK MYTHS

Greek Myths by Marcia Williams (Walker Books, 1994)

Greek Myths and Legends by Cheryl Evans and Anne Millard (Usborne, 1992)

The Iliad by Ian Strachan (Kingfisher, 1997)

The Iliad and the Odyssey by Homer and Marcia Williams (Walker Books, 1998)

Myths and Civilization of the Ancient Greeks by Hazel Mary Martell (Franklin Watts, 1998)

Tales of the Trojan War by Kamini Khanduri (Usborne, 1998)

CD-ROMs

Ancient Greece (Granada Toolkit Support Pack, Granada Learning, 2002)

Ancient Greece (Heinemann Explore History KS2, Heinemann)

Ancient Greece (Interfact Series, Two-Can Publishing, 2002)

Ancient Greeks (Anglia Multimedia Ltd, 1998)

Athenian Life: an adventure in Ancient Greece (4Mation Publishing, 2000)

DVD

Lost Treasures of the Ancient World - Ancient Greece (Cromwell Productions, 2003)

VIDEO

Hoplite Warfare – Warfare in Ancient Greece (Cromwell Productions, 1994)

Index